How

Choose a Career:

A Proven Method for Finding a Job You Will Love

By Patrick Grattan

Table of Contents

Preface

"Lieutenant Dan got me invested in some kind of fruit company. So then I got a call from him, saying we don't have to worry about money no more. And I said, that's good! One less thing." -Forrest Gump

If you are nearing high school graduation or thinking about a mid-career change, I hope you can appreciate the *awesome* decision you have before you: What profession do I want to enter into? Now, I don't mean "awesome" as in "cool" (though you may be excited at the possibilities), but rather I mean *overwhelming*! Do you realize there are billions of types of jobs in the world? How many have you considered so far? I'm guessing just a fraction, if any at all.

Even if you are coming into this book with a few careers in mind that you think would be good for you, in the first few chapters I'm going to urge you to be creative and open your mind to exploring more possibilities. Please don't limit yourself to preconceived notions about which career you should pursue. I want you to generate a list a mile long of career options including some you may not even currently be aware of. It is important to expand your mind like this so that you don't overlook what may be your best career fit.

Once you have an "awesome" list to choose from, how do you decide among the options? Some people go with their gut and decide emotionally. Others expect a quiz or guidance counselor to pick for them. Still others just go wherever the wind blows them. All these methods are like spinning a wheel and hoping for a satisfying outcome. Don't you dare do it! There is too much time, money, and happiness at stake to just leave your odds of a successful and fulfilling career to chance. Instead, in the last half of this book, I will show you a more analytical approach that you can use to narrow down your list into just a couple of professions that you can actively pursue. Even if you are a completely creative person that has never passed a math test in your life, it will be easy because I'm going to walk you step by step through the process to show you how to match your talents with a great career.

No person, book, or quiz alone can tell you what career you should take up; only you can decide, but that doesn't mean you have to go through the decision process alone. This book is going to take you step by step through a proven process that will creatively expand your mind followed by logically narrowing those options down into an ultimate career choice. That doesn't mean that the process will be quick, as it will require some thought and reflection; but, if you follow along, the process in this book is going to save you a lot of time, money, and happiness in the long run by leading you to a job you will truly love.

Let's get started!

Chapter 1

What Do You Want to Be When You Grow Up?

Five Popular Pieces of Bad Advice You Need to Ignore

"All children, except one, grow up." –Peter Pan

What do you want to be when you grow up? In elementary school, many children are asked this question to see what they will say. It's funny to hear their answers. When my brother was asked, he always said that he wanted to be a cardinal. No, not the Catholic kind, the avian kind! It's funny how our answer to this question evolves during youth. For me, I never really took it seriously until someone asked me with a straight face my freshman year in high school. I suddenly realized that the response I had given my whole life might not be the direction I really wanted to take. I always had said that I wanted to be the guy that pushed the start button for the rides at the carnival! Come on; think how much fun that would be to bring joy to people's lives!

I realized that by the time my high school senior year rolled around, people no longer asked with a smile on their face, they really want to know the answer. Perhaps you too are in this boat or are thinking about a mid-career change and asking yourself this question. In either case, you might have realized that not only do you not have a serious answer, but you don't even know how to arrive at a thoughtful answer.

Working for only one company for 30 years and then retiring is an obsolete mindset previous generations before us held. Recognize that as your life progresses you will grow and change as will the labor market. These days it is not unusual for people to change jobs several times during their working life. To prepare for such situations, it is more important than ever before that everyone have a solid method for identifying and matching their interests and talents to available careers. In upcoming chapters, I'm going to walk you through such a method. This method has worked incredibly well for me and will work for you too if you follow along with it. But first, let's look at five pieces of bad advice floating around out there that are quite common and unhelpful.

I remember when I was in high school and struggling to pick my first career. One of the things I would hear quite often from parents and teachers is "don't worry about deciding on a career; it will come to you". Umm, but that really isn't helpful. Going about your life without taking the time to really investigate career paths simply wastes valuable time. Perhaps I was supposed to meditate on it until the universe inspired me? Who knows. All I know is that this sort of career advice doesn't work because the suggestion "it will come to you" is not a structured process designed for success. Though in retrospect, I'm not sure this was ever serious advice. I think most people just have no idea what to tell you. This isn't a question with a black or white, yes or no, one-size-fits-all fixed answer.

The difficulty I had in trying to answer the question "What do you want to be when you grow up?" was also compounded by the fact that everyone liked to give me this second piece of bad advice: "You can be anything you set your mind to." I'm sure you have heard someone give this "helpful" advice too, but the problem with this saying is that it doesn't help you focus your choices. It actually has the reverse effect of making the possibilities overwhelming. If you take this advice to heart you could be setting yourself up for failure. Let's start this book right off by debunking that myth now: NO, YOU CAN'T BE ANYTHING YOU WANT.

Sure, in our modern world, we have the option to set our mind to anything we want, but will it result in success? Let me tell you that finding success in a career path depends mainly on whether you have passion and drive for it, whether you have the skills and talents for it, and whether or not a robust job market for it even exists. Without these characteristics, failure is more than likely. We will dive more deeply into these concepts in the next few chapters; but, before we do, I want you to think about what being successful in a career means to you. After all, if you don't define your goals, it will be difficult to achieve them.

What is your vision of a successful career? When I have asked people in my own life, the bad advice I usually get is "Do what you love. Do what you are passionate about." While this sounds nice and may even work out for you if you love investment banking, what about the guy or gal who only wants to play video games all day? That poor person's life may not be filled with all fun and games, ironically!

I remember a couple years back when I was at a fishing show and met one of the pro fishermen there who was putting on a fishing tips seminar. I thought: Now there is a guy living the dream, doing what he loves for a living....or so I thought. Talking to him I learned that turning pro made the sport he loves resemble something called "work." He explained to me that he used to fish for fun and as a way to relax and de-stress but when he decided to turn pro, all that went out the window. Fishing became stressful as he had to constantly perform at a high level to gain and maintain sponsors. He had to go out on the lake even when it was freezing, raining, and just plain miserable. Although he used to enjoy kicking back with friends on a boat, he now would rather spend his free time off the water. And, although he isn't a fan of writing or public speaking, he now is required to give seminars and write articles to make ends meet. In short, being a competitive sport fisherman sucked all the passion out of him for the sport. I learned from him that sometimes hobbies are best left as hobbies.

The fourth bit of bad advice I get from people (particularly from those that have experienced job loss) is that you need to find a career that ensures job stability and high earnings. Please realize though, that you will be spending about two thirds of your waking hours at work over the course of 40 or 50 years. What is going to motivate you to get out of bed every day? Money alone won't do it. Choosing an occupation just for money, without having passion for your work, will eventually lead to discouragement. I recall a buddy of mine in college that went into engineering, not because he particularly liked the field, but because the pay was decent. After a couple of years, he realized he just couldn't take the inactivity involved in sitting behind a computer in a basement lab 8+ hours a day. After much deliberation, he finally joined the military to find some excitement; and, to this day, he couldn't be happier!

Clearly, just doing what you love or just aiming for financial prosperity alone does not generate success. Instead, it's a combination of the two. So, how do you discover a career that will include a good balance of money and happiness that will ultimately lead to success? Although there is no way of knowing for sure, you can certainly put the odds in your favor by following the method presented in this book.

I can tell you that what puts the odds OUT of your favor though, is looking to others to tell you what profession you should choose. I know people who have gone into the same profession as their parents blindly assuming that the talents of their parents were passed down to them. I know people who simply went into whatever their guidance counselor recommended, not even considering if there might be something better for them. There are some who rely on an aptitude test thinking that answering 50 to 100 questions will guarantee a dream job. Don't get me wrong, parents, guidance counselors, and aptitude tests are valuable resources that will substantially aide you on your search. Just don't limit yourself to what someone else tells you. If you do, you may miss out on something much better.

In the end, only you can decide what career path is best for you. The more time and research you put in, the higher your chances of success. As you can probably guess, this will take some work on your part. However, if you follow along over the next couple chapters and do the homework, the insights you gain will pay dividends in your future.

Chapter Summary

• "What do I want to be when I grow up?" is now a serious question that requires a thoughtful answer.

• You are never too young or too old to consider this question and make course corrections since you and the world are ever changing.

• <u>MOST</u> people have no idea how to approach this subject and, as a result, issue bad advice.

• Bad Advice #1: Think about your options, the best choice will just come to you.

• Bad Advice #2: You can be anything you want to be.

• Bad Advice #3: Just do what you love.

• Bad Advice #4: Only choose high paying jobs with job security.

• Bad Advice #5: Your parents/ guidance counselor/ aptitude test will dictate the best path for you.

• A successful career can be achieved through finding a job in which you have the necessary <u>skills</u> and <u>talents</u> for paired with a strong <u>passion</u> and <u>drive</u>…. not to mention that the job needs to <u>exist</u> and be able to <u>pay the bills</u>!

Action Steps

• Finding the right career requires some work on your part so don't move on to the next chapter until you have gathered some <u>paper,</u> <u>sticky notes</u> and a <u>pencil</u>.

• **Seriously, don't go on until you have gotten those three things!**

Chapter 2

What Are Your **Talents**?

Five Unique Approaches to Uncover
Your Hidden Talents

"That was the most ghastly thing I've ever heard"
–Simon Cowell

You might want to be the next Justin Bieber or Jennifer Lopez; but if you don't have the singing talent, it isn't going to happen no matter how dedicated your pursuit. The weak man won't be successful at demolition; the ill-tempered woman won't be successful at waitressing; the impatient guy shouldn't be babysitting; and an astronaut prone to motion sickness will never exist. Although there may be something you love and are truly passionate about, a lack of talent in that area will prevent you from achieving high levels of success and reaching your income potential. If you are engaged in work that you love but are struggling financially to make ends meet, your passion will no longer be fun and rewarding but stressful and discouraging.

Some people select their career based solely on how impressive a job sounds or on which profession makes the most money. Unfortunately, those criteria alone will not ensure happiness. How happy can you be if you are performing subpar work every day? Think about it; would you rather be a mediocre cardiac surgeon or a superb kitchen designer? How about a second-rate bridge engineer versus an outstanding teacher?

So, what are your talents? Everyone has them but not everyone takes the time to actually identify them. By identifying your talents, you will be able to more easily recognize which specific professions align with your abilities. Take a moment to think about it. What talents are you aware of? What immediately comes to mind? Get out your sticky notes now and on each one start by writing one talent that you have. Do not skip this step. For this method to be successful, it is imperative that you take the time and effort to write down your talents before moving on to the next step.

Once you have written down all of your talents that come immediately to mind, let's try to uncover some hidden talents. One way to do this is by thinking about subjects in school you received high grades in and the achievements you accomplished in those classes. Were you able to climb the rope in gym class? Did you make an awesome tic-tac-tow board in wood shop? Did you help other students in math? Think through the subjects you took, you might surprise yourself to realize what you were good at. Once you've identified your achievements, consider the talents and abilities that helped you to successfully accomplish those tasks. Was your tic-tac-toe board awesome because you are good at measuring twice and cutting once? Or did it look great because you have a knack for design? Or was your success due to your strong attention to detail? Take a few minutes to write down the skills and talents that enabled you to excel in those tasks. If you have trouble identifying your talent, then just write down the activity itself for now.

Now, let's expand beyond our talents to include people skills. Some people are very good at interacting with others, while some are not. Either way, relating with others is important since we all need to deal with people in our daily lives. Think about the people skills you have by considering the following questions. Do you like meeting new people? Are you friendly and warm? Are you sensitive to other's emotions? Are you good at helping a friend through their problems? Do you have the patience to explain a smart phone to your grandfather? Are you able to effectively resolve conflict? Are you skilled in debating? Do you like to be a problem solver? Although this is not an exhaustive list, I think you get the picture. Doing these types of things effectively are absolutely valuable talents that can help you achieve success within various careers. Reflect on this for a while and write down your relational strengths. I want you to end up with a big stack of filled sticky notes by the end of this chapter.

Next, think about your soft skills. Soft skills differ from talents (or hard skills) in that they typically relate to the tools or methods you use to get a job done rather than the skills directly required for the task at hand. For instance, soft skills that might help you complete an activity could include strengths in public speaking, writing, negotiation, keeping an optimistic attitude through adversity, hard work ethic, team work, time management, conflict resolution, high self-confidence, computer literacy, leadership abilities or any of a number of others. Perhaps the fact that you are reading this book means you are good at planning, researching, organization and/or decision-making. If you can identify with any of these, be sure to write them down. While you are doing this exercise, I want you to also be aware of the soft skills you are not so good at. For all talents, but for soft skills in particular, you can and should develop them further throughout your life. Know that job seekers with stronger soft skills will often be chosen for a job position over other candidates not only when their backgrounds are otherwise equivalent, but in a lot of cases despite having a lower GPA. This is because soft skills are a critical asset in the workplace and as such need to be continually developed throughout your life.

The development of soft skills and deriving value from our thinking is more important today than it ever has been before. Historically, the value a person could produce for a company was based mainly on his/her ability to accomplish a certain number of tasks in a certain amount of time (such as how many widgets one can produce per day). Back then, competition for those jobs was limited to local job seekers only. Today, however, competition is fierce with jobs being outsourced to Mexico, China, India, and other low wage countries. With competition now at a global level, it is important to recognize that to justify a relatively higher wage we must create additional value for our employers through our thinking. For example, can you sell, save, devise, invent, prepare, plan, negotiate, present, write, build, manage, direct, organize, oversee, design, locate, coordinate, provide, train, or market something? Enhancing these skills will allow you to compete and win in the global market place. So, if you are proficient in these skills, be sure to write them down on your sticky notes.

I learned first-hand about the importance of soft skills and value added thinking while working at a grocery store bakery early on in my working life. There, the old mindset that a quantity of repetitive tasks was the only value the workers could produce was well entrenched. In that bakery, each worker had a single product that was their responsibility alone: one person made the bread, one person made the pastries, one baked the cookies, another decorated the cakes, and so on. When I was hired, I assumed these bakers would train me in their specialties. Was I ever wrong! I found that each employee was fiercely protective of the good that they made and would go so far as to stand in corners of the room so that no one else could see how they prepared their specialty. These employees mistakenly thought that their specialty alone made them irreplaceable to the store and that they could maintain job security as long as they kept their recipes a secret. What the store actually would have valued more was bakers who could focus more on customer's needs, provide inventive new desserts using existing ingredients, find cheaper ways to produce the same quality, experiment with dessert presentations to increase sales, and at a minimum, cross-train one another so that if someone is sick the store isn't out of bread that day. As I was leaving that job, the trend in the industry began shifting toward desserts that were pre-made in a factory. The desserts were frozen and shipped to the store where they were thawed and placed on a shelf. As a result, many bakery workers were let go. And no wonder, the lack of soft skills displayed by these employees made them easily replaceable by a machine. Whatever job you end up taking, remember that the value you create from your mind is far more important than the value that comes from your hands.

Continuing with your sticky notes of skills and talents I want you to next think back for a minute to identify what you were doing the last time someone told you "nice work", "I wish I could do that", or "wow, you did that fast!". There might be gifts here you could identify as well. People usually only say these things when someone displays a talent that isn't typical of the general population. These are times from which you should take note.

If you start to slow down in coming up with new talents, feel free to recruit others to help you brainstorm. You may have talents that come so easily to you that you overlook them, yet are obvious to others around you. Parents, spouses and close friends are great resources since they know you better than anyone else. Ask them "What am I good at?",

"What are my strengths?", "What activities do I excel at?" Their responses may surprise you.

Finally, I always like to flip it towards the end to consider the question from a different perspective: What are you terrible at? We tend to gravitate toward activities that utilize our abilities and avoid those that do not. If you totally suck at art, maybe that means you are good at organization and structure. If you loathe getting your hands dirty it may mean you are stronger at visualizing ideas. Some people hate getting bogged down in details, perhaps they are more big-picture goal oriented types. Think of some weak areas in your life and flip it.

Chapter Summary

• Everyone has talents, though, they are not always obvious. Focusing on different parts of your life can help you discover them.

• Focus Area #1: What school subjects are you good at?

• Focus Area #2: What people personality traits do you have?

• Focus Area #3: What are your soft skills? Thinking abilities?

• Focus Area #4: What do other people think you are good at?

• Focus Area #5: Identify your weaknesses and flip it to discover further talents.

Action Steps

• Consider each focus area and write as many of your talents as you can think of on individual sticky notes.

• When you begin to run out of ideas, recruit a parent, spouse or close friend to help you brainstorm.

• Keep these sticky notes somewhere safe, you will want to use them later to build your resume.

Chapter 3

What Do You Enjoy?

Five Ways to Determine Your Passion

"We're a couple of misfits" –Rudolph

Just because you are good at something doesn't necessarily mean you enjoy doing it. For example, you might be good at dealing with stress but that doesn't necessarily mean you want to be responsible for the lives of other people as an air traffic controller. If you don't enjoy what you do daily, you will become miserable and will likely make the people around you miserable as well.

Continue with your sticky notes by writing things you enjoy. You may have a list right off the top of your head, so start with those first. Think about what activities you would do if you had no responsibilities. How would you spend your days? Especially try to identify the aspect of each activity that makes you really enjoy it. For example, if your passion in life is burning ants with a magnifying glass, the aspects that you might write down may include "fire", "science", "experiments", "power" or whatever it is your twisted mind enjoys about it.

It may be useful to think about school or places you have worked. What did you enjoy about the time that you spent there? Talking to people? Helping, teaching, or coaching others? Fixing things, troubleshooting, or problem solving? Organizing or leading? You could simply write things like music, art, or football but again, if you can understand what exactly it is you like about those activities, it will be more beneficial later.

Also think about activities that make you happy and confident; activities that make time fly. What is it that you like about those activities? Personally, I enjoy video games, particularly real time and turn based strategy games. So, on my sticky note, I listed "resource management" and "strategy" as the enjoyable aspects of that activity.

Another way to explore your interests is to think about which magazines you are drawn to. What articles do you read? What have you "liked" on Facebook? What conversations perk up your ears when you hear them? For my brother-in-law, nothing turns him on more than politics. He eats and breathes it and his passion for politics has led him to get quite involved to the point that he has made a positive difference in the world.

Along those same lines, let's flip it. What annoys you? Is there something in this world that makes you mad?

Frustrated? How about environmental pollutants, poverty, political controversies, education, cancer or agnostics? Your fervor for such issues can be channeled in positive ways that can make the world a better place.

How is your stack of sticky notes coming along? Are you having trouble still coming up with things you like to do? Perhaps you need to step out of your comfort zone to better know yourself. Try challenging yourself to try new things. You'll never know for sure if you like something unless you try it. Here's a quick bucket list: have you ever ridden a horse? Been sky diving? Broken a board in a martial art? Been scuba diving to a shipwreck? Volunteered at a crisis center? Played a game of paintball? You may surprise yourself at your abilities, the aspects of these activities that you are good at, and what stirs your passions.

By now I hope you have a pretty good stack of hastily scribbled sticky notes. Spread them all out on a table and take a look at what you have. We are now going to make an affinity diagram which is just a fancy term for grouping the sticky notes into similar categories. Go ahead and try to combine them into just a few similarly themed groups.

Check out the following examples. As you look through them, you will notice that they are grouped based on similarities, but that the associations can be somewhat vague.

Group 1

Creating
Things   Art

Music

Explaining   Math
Stuff   Playing
with
Group 2 Children

Group 3   Fixing
Mountain Things
Biking
Wood
Shop

The goal here is to take your many talents and interests and to put them together in more manageable chunks that you can wrap your head around. As you look at the above examples though, it may not be clear to you why I grouped them the way that I did. In fact, you may very well have grouped them altogether differently; and that's okay, as long as the groupings make sense to you.

For instance, I matched "math" with "playing with children" since I was thinking of a classroom full of children having fun learning math. You might have paired "math" with "art" if you were visualizing beautiful architecture. Someone else might have combined "math" with "fixing things" if they were thinking about applying technical solutions to difficult problems. There are no wrong ways to put them together but it is important to consolidate your sticky notes into just a few groups as it will help you later to focus on just a few career fields.

Chapter Summary

• Life is long so you better enjoy your work. You can identify your passions by focusing on different parts of your life.

• Focus Area #1: What do you do in your spare time?

• Focus Area #2: What school or work activities do you enjoy?

• Focus Area #3: What are you doing when time just seems to fly?

• Focus Area #4: What magazines, websites, or conversations are you drawn to?

• Focus Area #5: Flip it, what is the opposite of what you hate?

Action Steps

• Consider each focus area and write as many of your interests as you can think of on your sticky notes.

• Group somewhat similar notes together so that all of them fall into just a few categories.

• If your list is short, challenge yourself to explore new interests.

Chapter 4

What Are Your Career Options?

Five Perspectives for Exploring New Careers

"May the odds be ever in your favor" –Hunger Games

In this chapter, we are going to start looking for some potential career paths that may be a good fit for you. Before we do that, I think it is important to point out how human physiology should play a role in your career selection process.

While talents and skills are unique to each individual person, "hemisphere dominance" of the brain splits all humans into basically two groups. You see, humans have two brain hemispheres: the left hemisphere and the right hemisphere. The left hemisphere is responsible for logic, analysis, and objectivity; while the right hemisphere is responsible for creativity, subjectivity, and intuitiveness. Just as some people are right-handed or left-handed, people can also be classified as "right-brained" or "left-brained". To some degree, one hemisphere will tend to be more dominant than the other and it is this hemisphere that we go to first for problem-solving.

There is an upside and a downside to brain hemispheric dominance as it relates to our career. First the upside: pretty much all jobs require either predominately right-brained or left-brained thinking as a foundation for success. Therefore, it is vitally important that we recognize which hemisphere is dominant so we can select jobs that utilize that side of the brain more. This is the most important step in finding a job that will fit you.

To pick the right career, there is no substitute for knowing yourself really well. Personally, I am very much left brained. Fortunately, I recognized this at a fairly early age, if by no other reason than the fact that I was getting A's in high school biology, trigonometry, and physics and C's in art, English, band, and psychology. That kind of gap in achievement is like a big flashing sign and I was lucky that my father recognized this and pointed it out to me so I could focus my efforts toward left-brained courses and career options. During my senior year of high school, I explored this new revelation about myself by taking classes in drafting, computer-aided design (CAD), and computer programming – all of which I excelled at and confirmed I had picked the right direction.

Although there was an extreme disparity between my brain hemispheres, hemispheric dominance is not always obvious. To help you recognize what type of thinker you are, answer the following questions.

1) When someone asks you what kind of car they should buy, is your first thought to suggest the hottest car around; or the most dependable?

2) If you are having a problem, is your first thought to think about who would be the most skilled to help you solve it; or do you try to figure it out yourself?

3) When starting a project, do you like to begin working on the biggest most important part first; or do you start by making a schedule/outline and preparing for or researching more about the task?

4) If someone is showing you a dance move, would you prefer that they teach you by performing it for you; or by verbally explaining it to you step by step?

If you picked the first answer for each question, this may indicate that you are a right-brained creative thinker rather than a left-brained analytical thinker.

Another way to figure out where you fall on the left-brained/right-brain spectrum is to study the following puzzle. Take a sheet of paper and make nine dots on it, as shown below. What is the fewest number of straight lines needed to connect all nine dots without picking up your pencil? Refer to the end of the chapter for the answer.

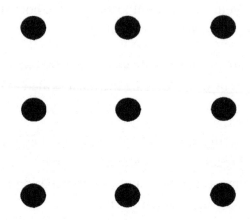

As you can see from my personal example, a strongly dominant brain hemisphere can be advantageous when it comes to narrowing your career options down to those that require that type of thinking at the foundational level. Disregarding or opposing your innate physiological tendencies will only put you in an unnecessary uphill struggle in your professional life. We need to put our nature to our advantage.

Interestingly, the second consequence of having a dominate brain hemisphere is a downside that can work against us if we aren't careful. While all jobs are basically analytical or creative in nature in which your brain type needs to be aligned with, you will never reach the highest levels of that profession if you don't develop some ability on your non-dominant side. For instance, a finance major working for a company in purchasing might do well if he is left-brained; however, if he is promoted to manager without having developed much of his right-brained thinking, he may fail in figuring out how to manage, motivate, and inspire his team. Or, take a right-brained artist who is scraping together a living by painting. If she develops her left-brained ability to program websites, her combined skills could make her wildly successful as a web designer.

The good news is that regardless of how far to the left or right we are on the creative/logic scale, we can always improve our non-dominant side through exercise. Just like exercising muscles improves strength, exercising the mind improves brain power. Creative endeavors for the "lefties" and logic puzzles for the "righties" are just some of the ways you can exercise your mind. If you do, it will be like building a second box of tools you can resort to for solving the problems that come up at your job and in your life.

A great example of how powerful a combination of left-brained/right-brained thinking can be is the career selection process described in this book. Selecting a suitable career is much more effective when we combine our left-brained and right-brained thinking into a single process. As you will see, we do this by first creatively brainstorming as many career path options as we can so that we don't overlook any great ones followed by logically narrowing those careers down to find which are the best fit for us. Combining these two types of thinking into a single process like this is going to bring far more success than if we rely on just one type of thinking. As we go through this process, continue to evaluate yourself by considering which you find easier, the creative expansion of ideas or the analytical task of narrowing them down.

Let's start now with the first part of creatively brainstorming as many career paths that align with our dominate brain hemisphere as we can. Now that you have grouped your sticky notes of talents and interests into just a few categories, we are going to try to come up with as many professions as we can that could be a match for most of the sticky notes in each grouped category. Take a single sheet of paper and along the left side start by setting aside room for each category and then list as many different careers as you can think of that could somewhat fit under each one.

Careers	Group 1	Group 2	Group 3
	Musician	Technical Writer	Trainer
	Graphic Designer	Juvenile Probation Officer	Bicycle Retail Sales
	Website Designer	School Teacher	Mechanic
	Tattoo Artist		Carpenter

When I help others through this process and younger people in particular, I usually find this part to be the most difficult for them. Determining your talents and interests is somewhat easy because it simply relies on inward reflection. Identifying career options that can match those traits, however, can be more difficult if you don't have enough life experience to have been exposed to all the various occupations in the world or know exactly what those jobs may entail. When thinking about existing jobs, we tend to only think about the jobs that our parents and neighbors have or the jobs that people in television sitcoms have and the jobs we can see in the world around us like waiters, landscapers, cashiers, and truck drivers. But this is an extremely limited view, and it can be hard see beyond our personal sphere of perception.

One of the best resources for me when I was in high school was the Federal Bureau of Labor Statistics. (I know, snore!) But actually, for a government entity, they have a pretty good website. Check out their website at http://www.bls.gov/ooh/ and look up a few of the careers you already have on your list. For each job check out the headings "What _____'s do", "Work Environment", and "Similar Occupations". This will help you to confirm if what you know about each job is really how it is. If you bounce around the site long enough, you will probably learn about new and interesting careers you had not heard of before. For now, ignore the 'Pay' and 'Job Outlook' headings. We'll get back to those in the next chapter. Take some time now to really explore this site. While you are at it, also check out http://www.onetonline.org/ for some more ideas. You could spend all day there, so put down this book now and investigate for a while.

If you have access to a guidance counselor, this may be a good time to consult with him/her, as they may be able to identify possible career paths for your list. Be sure to inform them of your talents, passions, and brain hemispheric dominance, so he/she can more effectively assist you in finding appropriate careers for you to investigate. Aptitude tests are also beneficial, so you may want to take one of those. An online aptitude test can be found at http://www.keirsey.com/sorter/register.aspx. Just don't get caught up in the guidance, we are only using these resources to brainstorm potential careers; we are not using them to pick one out.

Every year, certain publications come out with their lists of the "best" careers. These can be another great place to brainstorm possible positions. Check out http://money.usnews.com/careers/best-jobs/rankings/the-25-best-jobs. Again, remember to use these resources only to obtain ideas, not to single out a career. Because of this, "job rank" is completely irrelevant, and very much useless since these "best" jobs are not necessarily the best jobs for you. In the upcoming chapters in this book, we will be able to decide the best job for you based upon your unique talents and interests, not based on a "best job list" made by some guy using arbitrary criteria.

One more method you can use to open your eyes to professions you don't see every day is to make a "mind map" of all the jobs required to produce a simple ordinary product. This method occurred to me after reading the classic essay: "I,

Pencil" by Leonard E. Read. The essay itself is really quite engaging and makes some deep philosophical points. If you are interested, you can read it at:

http://www.econlib.org/library/Essays/rdPncl1.html. But let me adapt it for our own use.

On a new sheet of paper, write the words "Cedar Tree" on the left and "Pencil" on the right. From there, draw lines from cedar tree to pencil and make a box for each profession that is required to produce and sell that pencil from beginning to end. As you do this, you will be amazed at all the jobs that are required to produce such a simple object. Along the way, you may even recognize options you hadn't considered before. Check out my feeble attempt below.

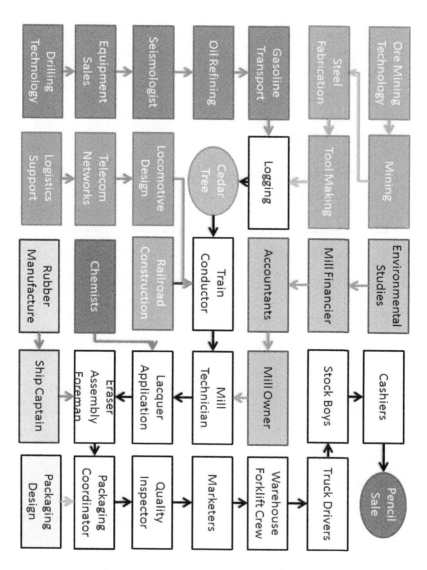

A basic attempt at listing the jobs required to make a pencil. I bet you could come up with many more.

Phew, that's a lot of jobs, and yet this just barely scratches the surface of all the jobs it takes to create the simplest of objects: the pencil.

Chapter Summary

• Determine careers that could match some, most, or all of the talents and interests in each sticky note grouping.

• Career Source #1: Federal Bureau of Labor Statistics http://www.bls.gov/ooh/

• Career Source #2: Guidance counselors.

• Career Source #3: Aptitude tests.

• Career Source #4: Annual job ranking lists by news outlets.

• Career Source #5: Mind map relating to the fabrication of specific products.

Action Steps

• List each career in a column along the left side of a sheet of paper.

• Take the time to determine your brain hemisphere dominance (logic vs. creative) and focus on careers that will align with it.

• To reach the highest levels of success, exercise your non-dominant brain hemisphere regularly.

Puzzle Answer:

Connect all nine dots with the fewest connected straight lines: So what is the fewest number of required lines? Did you come up with a left-brained answer like five? Or did you recognize that you didn't have to stay within the nine-dot "box" and came up with a right-brained answer like four or better yet three? If you are extremely right brained, perhaps you realized that you could use scissors to cut the dots out and tape them all in a line so you could draw a single line through them!

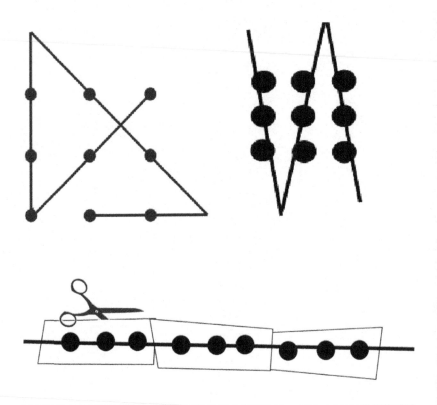

Chapter 5

What Jobs Does Society Need?

The Secret Relationship between Money and Happiness

"I'm Batman" –Batman

Yes, societal value is a factor! Job availability and corresponding pay are not set at random or by the kindness of corporate America; rather, they are set by the forces of *supply* and *demand*. That is to say, wages are set based on the *supply* of available workers with the requisite skills as well as the amount of *demand* or need for those workers.

Taken individually, a high supply of available workers for a given job tends to drive wages lower. Employers can lower wages and yet are always able to find someone who needs a job that is willing to accept that lower wage. On the other hand, low supply tends to have the opposite effect. With low available workforce, employers are forced to pay more to lure workers from other companies, fields, or geographic locations to fill the company's needs.

Demand is similar in that when a lot of companies need workers with unique or specialized skills, the wages will typically increase as they compete for the talent. Conversely, if companies have very little need for certain positions, or can get by without filling them at all, the company will tend to pay those jobs poorly rather than shell out a lot of money for marginally useful work.

What this boils down to is this: The going wage is an indication of how much mismatch exists between the pool of job seekers compared to the availability of jobs. One way this mismatch can work in your favor to produce higher wages, is when there is high consumer demand for a product but few workers that have the necessary skills to produce that product. Fundamentally, when society values a product, they are willing to pay more for it. This in turn provides for higher employee wages as companies compete to attract workers who can help them produce a profit by fulfilling society's need.

For example, the advent of smartphones has astounded consumers by the utility of apps; and the great hunger for these apps has driven demand through the roof. Apps are so new, however, that few app programmers exist, and those developers that do exist receive a high wage due to their scarcity. It's clear that at this time in history, society places a lot of value on app programmers as evidenced by the number of developers who have been made millionaires by their unique apps of utility. Once the market becomes completely saturated with app programmers, their value to society will diminish and their wages will settle down. Having an understanding about how wages are set is important when selecting a career since your income will be determined by the value society places on your work.

Take the case of the talented, passionate concert pianist. While society may say this type of music is valuable, the demand for it says otherwise. Society always puts its money into the things it values, and the fact is that people are not beating down the doors of orchestral halls with their wallets in hand. As a result, job availability is extremely low and extremely competitive. The same is true for radio/television announcers, reporters, actors, and rock bands among others. I'm not saying you should completely avoid these careers; just keep an open mind that there may be other careers that you find equally satisfying but with less competitive employment opportunities. When I was choosing my career, I found that I had interests in CAD drafting, computer programming, and engineering. I had talents in all three fields and derived equal enjoyment from each of them. So what was the tiebreaker for me? The average income made the choice easy.

So what is valuable to society? In other words, what does this world need more of? By examining wages, we can determine the answer. A low supply of skilled workers in fields of high demand will typically result in steady work at higher wages. An example of this is any job that requires a strong foundation in science and math. Today we are experiencing unprecedented demand for technology; yet, at the same time, the nation's schools are graduating teens with poor math and science skills. What evidence is there that this is actually happening? The fact that math- and science-based careers fetch above average wages confirm it.

How much importance do you place on income when selecting a career? Stop for a second and think about it. There are many preconceived attitudes about the importance of earnings. At one end of the spectrum, there are people who place high importance on finding work they will love without much regard for income. At the other end of the spectrum, are people who place their greatest emphasis on generating wealth, recognition, and power, regardless of how boring and unfulfilling the work might be. I'm not sure where you fall on this spectrum, but hopefully it is somewhere in between because the secret relationship happiness has to money is that income ought to be pursued with moderate emphasis.

At the one end, completely disregarding that a job is low paying in order that you might pursue something you are passionate about will lead to stress and anxiety about making ends meet. You may find yourself more unprepared for this reality than you might think. At the other end, solely pursuing money can lead to an unfulfilling life that is void of some of the special experiences and relationships that money can't buy. If you are predisposed even a little bit toward either end of this spectrum, then I urge you to work on changing your mindset. Only a moderate pursuit of income can lead you to a balanced life.

Depending on where you are in life, you may have a hard time keeping a balanced approach. This may be because our perspective tends to evolve over time as we get older. I have found that many young adults tend to underestimate the importance of a good income when it comes to selecting a career since they tend to be more idealistic and are less likely to place a lot of importance on money. Yet, as people grow older, their expenses tend to increase and they begin to recognize the importance of money when it comes to starting a family, paying for health care costs, and saving for retirement. Keeping a moderated perspective on income will keep you from recognizing too late in life that your planning has been insufficient.

If you tend to discount the importance of income, be doubly sure to take into consideration your long-term income requirements before choosing a career and, if necessary, develop a secondary career plan. If you tend to place more significance on income, recognize that it is more important to find a career that is a strong match to your talents and interests since those factors are essential to being truly successful. Money always follows success; so, if you focus on being successful, money will come. Maintaining a balanced, moderate view can be challenging; but it will become easy, as I will explain in the next chapter exactly how to factor it into your career selection decision with just the right amount of emphasis.

Okay, it's time to do some research. Don't worry; it won't be too painful. The link is http://www.bls.gov/ooh/. On the website, navigate to each career on your list and make a note of the median salary.

Chapter Summary

• A job's availability and wage are set by supply and demand as dictated by society's values.

• You do not have to agree with society's values, but you need to be aware of them and respect them.

• Moderate the importance you place on income: Having a disregard for a career's income can lead to stress and discouragement.

• Moderate the importance you place on income: Having an obsession for money can lead to an unfulfilling life.

Action Steps

• Note the median salary for each career on your list.

Chapter 6

How Does This All Come Together?

A Simple yet Powerful Tool You Can Use for a Lifetime

"Am I going mad, or did the word 'think' escape your lips? You were not hired for your brains, you hippopotamic land mass." –The Princess Bride

Okay, you right-brained people, bear with me as we have some left-brained fun, it's time to put it all together. To do that, we are going to use a tool called a Decision Analysis Chart which is a nerdy way of saying we are going to fill out a worksheet that will help us select a career. For simplicity's sake, let's call it a "Career Selection Table" or better yet let's just call it a "table," as it rolls off the tongue better. You can continue using the paper from the previous chapter that has your jobs listed down the left side of the sheet to make your own table or skip ahead to the last page of this book to find out how you can download a Career Selection Table Worksheet that is already formatted and ready to use.

The great thing about using this table is that it will help you organize your thoughts by providing a framework from which you can more logically and unemotionally balance your options. This is important when it comes to complex and/or emotional decisions since it can be difficult to objectively consider multiple factors simultaneously. As you make your table, you will notice how it breaks the decision down into smaller, easier-to-digest pieces. This will reduce the complexity while hiding the result until you have finished each piece of the evaluation. This will remove any emotional influence that might otherwise bias your analysis. Although emotion should play some role in your final decision, it can also blind you into making poor choices. This Career Selection Table is going to give you a purely analytical vantage point you wouldn't normally have otherwise.

Furthermore, I want to point out that the sole results of this table should not be used to make a career decision for you. Instead, it is meant to give you a more informed view so that you can better choose the best career for yourself. This table will provide valuable insights, but remember that it is only a framework that uses simplified inputs. Since your day-to-day thinking and priorities can change, the results you receive today may differ from the results you get tomorrow. Therefore, use this tool as a snapshot in time based upon your current thinking. When you receive new information or view a choice in a different light, you should rework the table to obtain a new answer.

The way this table works is by having you rate each career option according to how strongly your talents align with it, how much the career interests you, and by the average earnings in that field. For each career option, the categories are weighted equally and then added together for a final score.

This combination of ratings is a balanced approach to selecting the right career for a number of reasons.

1) I believe that a good income is only half as important as being successful at your job since money will typically catch up to those who are successful. Success usually results from high levels of engagement in your work in addition to having strong abilities (interest/passion + talent). Evenly weighing each of the three categories inherently sets the median income (income) half as strongly as passion and talent combined.

2) This configuration ranks interest (interest/passion) at the same level as talent and income to prevent us from choosing careers that risk leading us to boring and unfulfilling lives.

3) The category "Talents" includes not only talents but skills, since talents can cover a lack of skills and skills can cover a lack of talents.

4) Finally, the category "Interests" includes not only interests but passion, as interests and passion typically

go hand in hand. When you pursue something you enjoy, you will usually develop a passion for it.

To create your own table, start by drawing in five vertical lines to form a total of six columns. Label Column 1 "Groups", Column 2 "Careers", Column 3 "Talents", Column 4 "Interests", Column 5 "Income", and Column 6 "Total". Recall that "Talents" represent what you're good at or have skills in. "Interests" are what you enjoy or have passion for. "Income" will represent the median annual income, and "total" will represent the sum of columns 3, 4, and 5. See the following figure.

	Careers	Talents	Interests	Income	Total	
Group 1	Musician	8	10	1	19	👍
	Graphic Designer	5	6	4	15	👍
	Website Designer	4	5	8	17	👍
	Tattoo Artist	7	4	4	15	👍
Group 2	School Teacher	9	7	5	21	👍
	Juvenile Probation Officer	4	1	5	10	
	Technical Writer	8	7	6	21	👍
Group 3	Carpenter	6	8	4	18	👍
	Mechanic	4	4	4	12	
	Bicycle Retail Sales	7	7	2	16	
	Trainer	5	2	3	10	

For each career, you will now rate each category on a scale from 1 to 10 with 10 being the highest. The "Talent" and "Interests" columns will be subjective ratings that correspond with how closely your abilities and personality align with each career. The "Income" column, however, will be a fixed number found by taking the median annual income of each career and dividing by 10,000 and then rounding to the nearest whole number. For example, a median annual income of $75,000 would be rated as an 8 ($75,000 / 10,000 = 7.5 -> rounds to 8). Finally, on each row, add all three columns together and place the total in the last column.

Once your totals are calculated, you will clearly see which careers are comparatively a better fit for you. In our example, the top three careers options would be musician, school teacher, and technical writer.

As I previously mentioned, this type of analysis is just a framework to help you weigh the possibilities as the highest rated career might not actually be the best route. For instance, in the above example, musician is a career option this particular fictitious person is quite talented in and extremely passionate about. However, due to the low pay of this profession, its total score ranks just third out of all the career options on the list. Does this mean that this particular career option should be eliminated from consideration? Not necessarily, perhaps with a bit of creativity we can consider something better. For instance, if they were to combine school teacher and musician to get high school music teacher, we might find that it rates much more favorably. Another possibility might be teaching private music lessons during the evening while working a day job writing technical owners' manuals. Still another option might include a primary career as a musician while writing fiction novels on the side. A low rating does not necessarily mean that you need to eliminate that career from consideration, but may indicate a need to creatively explore other related career options based upon the data gathered from your table.

Finally, if there is a certain geographical location in the world where you want to live, add a couple bonus points to careers associated with industries with a large presence in that region. If you have family in the Midwest, you could bump up the points for careers associated with manufacturing. If you dream of surfing every day after work, plug a few more points in for technological careers so you can aim for Silicon Valley. Taking advantage of local industry will ensure that your pay is above the job's national average and will reduce the likelihood of unemployment in your working years. Trying to eke out a career without locally established associated industries will make life somewhere between tough to impossible.

Study your completed table and think about why the scores come out the way that they did. Consider how to combine different vocations, how the numbers would change depending on different geographical locations, as well as which careers should be relegated to hobbies. Doing so will set you up to make an informed final decision.

Chapter Summary

• The Career Selection Table provides a framework from which you can more logically and unemotionally weigh your options.

• This table provides a snapshot in time of your current thinking and must be reevaluated as you gain new perspectives.

• This table cannot decide your career direction but will inform it.

• Go with the flow and emphasize your geographically local industries.

• The Career Selection Table is a handy tool that can easily be adapted for evaluating any complex and emotional decision in your life.

Action Steps

• Skip to the last page of this book to download a preformatted Career Selection Table Worksheet.

• Determine a rating for each career from 1 to 10 with 10 being the highest under each heading.

• Talent Heading: Rate the combined strength of your talents, skills, and people personality.

• Interests Heading: Rate the combined level of your interest, enjoyment, and passion.

• Income Heading: Rate the income by rounding the first digit of the median annual salary.

• Add the three ratings together and list the answer under the "Total" heading.

• Careers with high point totals should be strongly considered and investigated further.

• Analyze the ratings that contributed to any surprise results.

• Try combining careers, emphasize industries in your geographic target location and decide if some careers would be better as a hobby for new point totals and leaders.

Chapter 7

What Other Factors Should I Consider?

Critical Final Considerations for Picking a Winning Industry

"Never tell me the odds!" –Hans Solo

I hope you have found the Career Selection Table to be as helpful for you as it has been for me with regard to identifying potential careers based on your talents and interests. If you have followed along and made your own table, you should now be able to easily narrow your choices down to just a few career paths for further investigation.

As you consider your top-rated careers, your next step is to study the state of the industry corresponding to each career option. This is an important step since the world is changing so fast these days that most industries go through some sort of major upheaval every decade or so as new technology emerges and consumer tastes change.

As you learn about these industries, think about where the future lies for them. A question you may ask yourself is if this type of job can easily be outsourced overseas to low wage countries? As companies have worked to become more profitable in order to stay competitive, jobs that involve repetitive tasks performed by unskilled labor were the first to be outsourced. With the advent of high speed internet, however, this outsourcing trend has been extended to any type of work done on the computer as well. You may have already noticed that when calling technical support hotlines, often your call is routed to overseas call centers as many companies have outsourced information technology analyst jobs to low wage countries. Other jobs that are prone to outsourcing may include fields pertaining to part design, finite element simulations, computer programming, human resources, accounting, payroll processing, and many others as well. While well-developed soft skills can give you an edge in maintaining your position within an industry, it may be better to pick a career from your table that is more difficult to be offshored like jobs in the service and technology industries.

It is important to try to predict where an industry is heading so you can best decide how to prepare for your career. During my junior year of college, many of my graduating friends accepted positions with sign-on bonuses which were being offered by hungry, expanding auto companies rushing to keep up with a growing economy. Yet, when I graduated from college just a little over a year later, a recession was in full effect and sign-on bonuses were a thing of the past. Instead, the norm was to attend crowded career fairs punctuated by long lines of job seekers waiting to speak with recruiters who weren't even accepting resumes. However, I recognized that what I was witnessing a cycle, not a trend, and that I just needed to wait it out. Instead of rushing out to change my career before I had even started, I decided to double down and attend graduate school, even though that wasn't part of my original plan. The bet paid off for me as just two years later, the auto industry was back in a full hiring swing again and I had a job offer from a major auto company right as I graduated.

If an industry isn't doing so "hot" right now, consider why that might be the case and try to ascertain if what you are seeing is part of a cycle or a larger trend. So far, capitalism has served as the best economic system to date; however, it does have its drawbacks. One of the hallmarks of capitalism are the "booms" and "busts" it goes through as consumer's tastes and technology rapidly change. As industries get "hot," there is an increase in demand for jobs in those fields which translates into higher wage offerings. The supply of employees with the requisite skills always lags behind meeting that demand as it takes longer to train workers for a given field compared to the speed at which the need for them arose. As those industries over expand, the consumer market becomes saturated with product. The bust then goes into full effect, corresponding job demand falls, and the job market is flooded with the unemployed that need to be retrained to enter a different field. This lag between fast demand changes and slow worker retraining pushes wages and job availability up and down.

Pretty much all industries are at least somewhat cyclic in nature; however, some industries experience quite drastic cycles on a regular basis. When an industry experiences a big run up or boom, it is sometimes also referred to as a "bubble" while the resulting bust is referred to as the bubble "popping". In the recent past we have seen bubbles grow and pop in many sectors such as the dot com bubble, the real estate bubble, and military bubble. Perhaps in the near future we will see the popping of the big government bubble, college tuition bubble, healthcare bubble, self-driving car bubble, and maybe even the green energy bubble in its current form. Figuring out whether a run up in an industry is a long-term trend or a bubble about to pop is not always easy but may be necessary for your career planning. There are two indicators which may suggest that an industry is experiencing a bubble rather than long term growth and you can see them in all the bubbles I just mentioned. Either the products are strongly overhyped or the government participates in one way or another within the industry. Looking for these two indicators can help you understand the state of the industry you are considering.

In addition to identifying short-term cycles, be sure to focus on long-term trends in the industry as well. Over the years, there have been some tectonic shifts in demand, in the way business is conducted, and in the products produced. For example, with the development of digital media, there has been a decline in the print publishing and music industries. The advancement of iPads and tablets seems to have spelled the death of the home PC industry. Large consolidated farms are replacing small individual farms; cell phones and the internet are replacing landline phone service, and the looming debt crises many nations face jeopardize the future of numerous government jobs. Changing times means that some jobs are becoming obsolete. Awareness of this economic reality is necessary to nimbly navigate the job market rather than get run over by it.

If you enter into a profession which is characterized by short-term cycles, you may be required to ride out the bad times and to set aside money during the good times. If this is the case, it is important to recognize it early so that you can be prepare and plan accordingly. On the other hand, if your industry is being stamped out by the wheels of progress, you need to acknowledge this so you can start transitioning into another occupation prior to the elimination of your job.

Lastly, you should always have a backup plan in the event you find yourself out of a job. Choosing a minor in college is one way to do this. Another is to be aware of all the professions you could enter into with a given degree. You can also think about linking your chosen profession with an unrelated one for a greater number of opportunities. For example, you could combine business with a foreign language or history with teaching. You could also pair real estate with interior decorating, finance with international export law, or an electrician with marketing. There are many possibilities. Many of these add-ons require only a few classes to obtain a certificate. Specializations like this will likely put you in high demand or at least open doors to other industries that would otherwise be closed to you.

I work with an engineer who had been employed at our company for many years. In 2000, he decided to take advantage of a booming real estate market by quitting his position, forming a crew, and building houses. His venture turned out to be a very profitable one. In 2008, however, the real estate market started to crash. At that time, he decided to reapply with our company. Not only was he rehired, but he was placed in management due to the skills he had acquired while managing a building crew. Having a backup plan enabled him to transition to wherever society needed him; he never had to worry about finding a job regardless of what the economy did and, not to be overlooked, he made a lot of money along the way.

Chapter Summary

• Booms and busts are characteristics of capitalistic societies and cause demand to change faster than workers can be retrained.

• Some industries experience more extreme cycles than others.

• Extreme cycles are called "bubbles" and usually have something to do with overhype of a product or government involvement in the industry.

• Knowing your industry allows you to prepare for downturns and adjust your career path ahead of long-term declines.

Action Steps

• Study the state of your prospective industry. Is it in long term decline? Headed for obsolescence? Is your potential job being outsourced overseas?

• Is your prospective industry experiencing a cycle that is typical of that industry? Will you have to wait it out or expect job loss during the next down cycle?

• If your prospective industry is prone to strong cycles or outsourcing, how will you improve you job security? Cross train in a different field? Work on obtaining outstanding soft skills? Graduate degrees? Make a plan or choose a different vocation.

• Even in stable industries you should always have a backup plan. Know all the jobs available to someone with the degree you are pursuing. Consider certificates in other somewhat unrelated fields as add-ons.

Chapter 8

What if I Still Can't Decide Which Career is Right for Me?

A Dependable Solution for the Undecided

"Git-R-Done!" –Mater

You are right to take your time to consider your options. Choosing a career is not something you should take lightly since the decision will have reverberating effects on the rest of your life. You need to make a thoughtful, insightful, and informed decision but don't let it paralyze you. You must decide on a career within a reasonable amount of time. If you are having trouble yet are sure you have the capability and means to attend college, then let me make this much clear:

DON'T PUT OFF GOING TO COLLEGE!

Putting off college for even a semester greatly increases the risk that you won't ever go. Even if you do eventually attend college, you may regret the time you had spent procrastinating, especially if it involves lost income that you could have earned as a professional.

If you aren't sure which college or university to go to, I would recommend attending a local community college. Doing so allows you to take classes from a variety of fields that will provide you with an overview of other careers. Not only will you be learning and gaining skills, but you'll be earning credits at reasonably priced rates that typically can be transferred later to other colleges and universities. There really isn't much of a downside to enrolling.

The benefits of community college are:

• *Chance to explore a variety of fields*

• Low cost

• Flexible classes allow you to work simultaneously

• Credits usually transfer to bigger universities

• Smaller class size

• Lots of academic support

Once you are able to narrow your career options to just a few majors, you should enroll at an accredited university that has good programs in those fields. Enrolling as an undeclared major is not unusual, just make sure you focus your first year on exploring your choices so that you don't string your college years and corresponding debt load out too much. Having said that, if you do decide on a major and at some point realize that a different major would be a better fit for you, don't hesitate to correct your ships heading immediately. Even if it does delay your graduation, it is important to be in the field that fits you best.

While you are enrolled, be sure to take the time to talk with people in the professions you are considering, read about the careers from different sources on the internet, visit the business, perhaps even intern/volunteer there for a while or shadow a professional within the industry.

When my wife was in college, she wasn't sure if becoming a probation officer was a good fit for her or whether she should pursue something else entirely. To help her decide, she called her local courthouse, explained her situation, and set up an appointment to meet with one of the probation officers in their office. It turned out to be an invaluable experience because although the internet could tell her hard facts and history about the profession, meeting the officer in his office enabled her to experience firsthand what working in a courthouse environment was like. Speaking directly to the probation officer, my wife learned not only about the discouraging aspects of dealing with probationers who become repeat offenders, but also the enjoyment of occasionally being able to help someone improve their life. Insights like these are only obtained through discussions with a professional in the field.

I strongly encourage you to contact a professional working in a field you are considering. You can find people like that through www.LinkedIn.com, through the professors at your school, or just call the business directly to make an appointment. At your meeting, be sure to listen carefully and let them do most of the talking. Also, be sure to use open-ended questions that will promote discussion and elicit useful information. Examples of such questions may include the following:

- Tell me what your typical day is like?

- What do you like and/or dislike about your job? Is your job rewarding? Repetitive?

- Does your job allow you to maintain a good balance between your work and your personal life?

- How many hours do you work per week? Does your employment require any late-night or weekend hours? Are you expected to work while you are at home?

- How much vacation/personal time off do you receive? Is there time off to care for sick children?

- What kind of education is required for this profession? Degrees? Certifications? Apprenticeships?

- How much and what kind of continuing education (Seminars, training, classes, etc.) does your job require? Does your employer pay for them?

• What opportunities exist for promotion? Where could this career take me? What other occupations exist for professionals with your skills?

Don't be shy about doing this, the majority of people out there will be more than happy to meet with you. People tend to like to talk about themselves and usually enjoy helping aspiring young professionals.

Once you have taken a few classes and met with a professional, reconstruct your Career Selection Table again without referring to the previous one. Your present results will most likely be quite different from your preceding ones as you have gained a more informed understanding of each of your career choices.

Chapter Summary

• It is normal to have a hard time deciding your career path.

• Don't give up! Continue to research careers through internet searches, visiting businesses, talking to people in various professions and taking internships.

• Community college can expand your horizons at bargain prices for credits that can usually be transferred to bigger schools.

Action Steps

• Don't put off college. Enrolling as an undeclared major is an option many people choose their first year.

• Spend a lot of time researching careers and be sure to rework the Career Selection Table as you gain new insights.

Conclusion

"You may not survive to pass this way again and these may be the last friendly words you'll hear." –Pirates of the Caribbean

The world is changing at an amazing rate, and you need to prepare yourself for the reality that you may need to change careers at least once in your lifetime. Mastering the ability to identify your changing interests and talents and matching them to ever changing career fields is a skill that the modern worker cannot be without.

I hope that the process outlined in this book has helped to shed some light on the best career fit for you. If it did, I would love to hear from you about your success at Patrick.D.Grattan@gmail.com. I hope that you have found this process easy to follow and that you've gained a good understanding on how to create the Career Selection Table. As you may have already recognized, this table can be adapted to analyze any major decision in life, such as which college to attend, which job offer to take, which house to buy or whether or not both parents should work.

Your decision about which career to enter into is one of the biggest decisions you will make in your life and will have lasting consequences for both you and the world around you. In this book, I have discussed considerations that will put the odds of a successful working career in your favor. Unfortunately though, no one can see the future and how things might turn out. The most important advice I can give you is to rely on God to guide you in His will. Consult with Him about your career planning, as He can bring success beyond your imagination, regardless of the situation.

"But seek first His kingdom and His righteousness, and all these things will be given to you as well." Matthew 6:33

I would wish you luck on your journey, but luck is merely the intersection of preparation and opportunity. If you have completed all the exercises in this book, then you have a huge leg up on preparation. From there, God will provide the opportunity; and you will be in position for a successful and fulfilling career.

About the Author

Patrick Grattan's Alma Mater was Michigan Technological University, where he earned a Bachelor and Master of Science degrees in Mechanical Engineering with emphasis on Solid Mechanics.

After graduation, he started his career at the Nissan Technical Center Safety Department in Farmington Hills, Michigan, where he designed, developed, and evaluated seatbelt and airbag restraints through computer simulations and live crash testing with instrumented test dummies.

In his spare time, he enjoys developing stock market trading strategies and in 2008, launched his own business www.RevereTrading.com to market his timing strategies to the public.

Freebie for My Readers!

Thanks for supporting my book. Customer's reviews on Amazon really help me out. If you are willing to write a review for me, let me know at Patrick.D.Grattan@gmail.com and I will send you a free Career Selection Table Worksheet that will help you with your career selection process.

To leave a review, go to: http://www.amazon.com/dp/B00A8UQWCC and scroll down the page to find the customer review section.

Customer Reviews

There are no customer reviews yet.

5 star	
4 star	Share your thoughts with other customers
3 star	**Write a customer review**
2 star	
1 star	

Thanks!
-Patrick

Made in the USA
Monee, IL
23 August 2020